FIGHTER AIRCRAFT
of the United States

by Terry Morgan

with scale drawings by Richard Groh

A Len Morgan Book

ARCO PUBLISHING COMPANY, INC.,
219 Park Avenue South,
New York, N. Y., 10003

Published by Arco Publishing Company, Inc.
219 Park Avenue South, New York, N.Y. 10003

Library of Congress Catalog Card Number 66-19792
Printed in U.S.A.

ACKNOWLEDGMENT

My thanks to those instrumental in the preparation of this book go to Richard Groh for his invaluable technical assistance, Col. C. V. Glines, Lt. William P. Campbell, Major Robert A. Webb, N. E. Taylor, Thomas R. Cole and Chester Chatfield of the Boeing Company, Dave Rottering of the Blue Angels, Ron Cook of North American Aviation, Robert T. O'Dell, James R. Harrell of Hayes International Corporation, A/2C Doug Guerette, Lt. Gale Lawson, Cmdr. R. S. Jones, Edward Regan of the McDonnell Aircraft Corporation, Vernon MacPherson of the Lockheed Aircraft Corporation, Arthur L. Schoeni of Ling-Temco-Vought, Incorporated, Victoria Vertichio of Republic Aviation Corporation, Major Francis N. Satterlee, Lt. Jerome Lagemann, Lt. Thomas Pelandini, Crosby Maynard of the Douglas Aircraft Company, Lt. Gerald F. Broening, Capt. Richard Barros, R. A. Hachten of the Northrop Corporation, Lt. Robert Glymph, Fred Bettinger of General Dynamics Convair Division, Harry Burns of the Grumman Aircraft Corporation, the Information Officers of the Air National Guard Units of South Dakota, North Carolina, South Carolina, Texas, Kansas, Ohio, Maryland, Illinois and Florida and my special thanks to my father, Len Morgan, who proved to me that anything is possible.

T.M.

The Glamour Boys

... of every air force have always been the fighter pilots. The pilots of those high-spirited, sleek and belligerent-looking machines have been the center of attention at every air show and the envied idols of every young boy since flight proficiency meant the difference between life and death.

As the airplane matured, so did the rules governing it until there came a day when the devil-may-care attitude embraced by pursuit pilots began to care. But the glory of those who appear to fearlessly challenge the sky to doubt their aerial abilities is still there. The pilots of the crack fighter squadrons of the sixties in their intricate computerized machines draw the same sparkle from the same eyes that watched over a barbed wire fence thirty years ago for a glimpse of a Curtiss Hawk.

Not only have the rules of the flying game changed a little since Dad was young, but the metamorphosis of the airplane is quite a few steps ahead of the pilot's willingness to accept it. Some of the same jockeys who escorted the Liberators and Flyingfortresses to and from Germany in their P-51s, P-47s and P-38s are in the cockpits of the most advanced interceptors flying today. The change from prop to jet, gunsight to computer, machine gun to missile and 400 miles per hour to Mach 2.5 is a technological advancement barely fathomable in just a scant twenty-year span. The machines have changed, but not their masters.

But now the military futurists say that they see the end of the manned fighter and the brink of the missile age for total defense. Mourning for the passing glory of a pilot who singly pits his aeronautical mastries against another might seem premature. It is becoming more and more obvious that the duties fulfilled by the fighter cannot be undertaken by guided missiles, no matter how advanced the art of rocketry. Possibly the fighter is an irreplaceable institution and its mere survival is dependent upon man not wishing to relinquish the human element that has been surpassed by his technology.

The fighter aircraft and the pilots who man them are in a world by themselves. Not disregarding the importance of the manned bomber, transport and aircraft of fine fettle, the emphasis has and always will be on speed and performance. Charles Yeager, the first man to travel supersonically, the X-15 pilots and their exploits on the threshold of space and most dramatically, America's astronauts — all teethed on fighter aircraft.

So has it been since the Montgolfier brothers built a fire under their magnificent balloon in 1783, fighter aircraft and the men who fly them are in the limelight of the airplane's dynasty. The glamour boys...

3

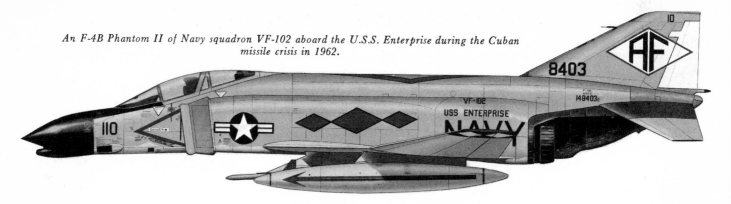

An F-4B Phantom II of Navy squadron VF-102 aboard the U.S.S. Enterprise during the Cuban missile crisis in 1962.

THE McDONNELL F-4 PHANTOM II

The most versatile and undoubtedly the most popular fighter in the armed services is the McDonnell F-4 Phantom II. Having the unique distinction of being one of the few fighters to have its inception aboard an aircraft carrier, the Phantom II is in active service today with all three branches of the military.

Development of the Phantom began in 1953 when the Navy Department contracted the McDonnell Aircraft Company of St. Louis to design and build a single-seat shipboard attack fighter. Before production began, the Navy revised their order for a high altitude interceptor relying solely on a missile fire control system.

Seeing that the specifications clearly called for the performance of two men, McDonnell stretched their design for another crewman and finalized the plans. The first aircraft entered service in 1958. Soon after, the Air Force took notice and 18 months later, they took their first delivery. The Marines followed suit.

The Phantom II incorporates a strictly functional design in that every exposed surface has a purpose in the overall performance of the machine. Little attention was paid to appearance in the bird's construction. Ideally adopted for aircraft carrier operations, the Phantom II features boundary layer control, a necessity for slow approaches to the deck.

In 1962, Air Force Col. R. B. Robinson and his radar

intercept officer set a new world's speed record in a Phantom II when they averaged 1,606.32 miles per hour in a three-way dash. Operable at ceilings above 60,000 feet, the Phantom II is armed with Sparrow radar homing air-to-air missiles and a number of combinations of bombs and rockets totalling 13,000 pounds.

Great Britain has placed orders for as many as 130 Phantoms to be delivered in 1969 and the Royal Canadian Air Force will use the Phantom II as the successor to their CF-104 Starfighters.

At Nellis Air Force Base, a McDonnell F-4C Phantom II of the 4520th Combat Crew Training Wing wheels in after a practice sortie.

6

Above: Near Edwards Air Test Center, an F4C Phantom II of the Tactical Air Command parallels the peaks of the Sierra Nevadas.

Left: Deck hands on the U.S.S. Enterprise volley up two Phantom IIs slated for simultaneous departures.

As the crew chief swings the chocks to the nosewheel, this Air Force jockey shuts down his Phantom II on the flight line at Nellis AFB.

Armed with its own definition of a big stick, this Phantom II walks softly in Air Force colors.

Off the coast of southern California, these Marine pilots head homeward to El Toro.

Laden with cameras for reconnaissance, the RF-4 Phantom II shoots at supersonic speeds and doesn't give anyone a chance to smile.

A McDonnell F-101B Voodoo from the 437th Fighter-Interceptor Squadron based at Oxnard Air Force Base in the autumn of 1964.

THE McDONNELL F-101 VOODOO

The McDonnell F-101 Voodoo never played the role for which it was cast. Designed and built to meet the specifications of the Strategic Air Command as an escort fighter for long-range bombers, the Voodoo completed flight trials at Edwards Air Test Center proving itself as a better fighter interceptor. Twin J57 Pratt and Whitney turbojets with afterburners give the F-101 an ideal climb rate exceeding 14,000 feet per minute for quick scramble and intercept missions.

Several variants of the single-seat high performance fighter were developed including the camera-laden reconnaissance model and a tandem seater for carrying a radar fire control officer. In service with the Air Defense Command, the two-seat F-101B incorporates the Falcon air-to-air missile in place of the 20 mm cannon used on the single-seat fighter version. The reconnaissance

RF-101C Voodo with its characteristic snub nose, was instrumental with the 363rd Tactical Reconnaissance Wing at Shaw Air Force Base in South Carolina in identifying Soviet missiles in Cuba in 1962.

With an operational speed of 1,200 miles per hour (Mach 1.2), the Voodoo is in current service with the U.S.A.F. Tactical Fighter Wings, Tactical Reconnaissance Wings, Air Defense Command, Air National Guard, the Royal Canadian Air Force and the Chinese Nationalist Air Force. For the most part, the McDonnell F-4C Phantom II is reequipping U.S.A.F. units currently staffed with the Voodoo.

Midway through the production of the initial orders placed for the Voodo, a modification was initiated to render the aircraft adaptable for yet another role. Structural strengthening and provisions for nuclear crutches

13

were added to make the Voodoo suitable for low-level close support operations.

Having the distinction of being the first McDonnell aircraft to capture a world's speed record, the F-101 is still in active interceptor squadrons commanding the same respect as the day it was placed in service. As an early warning interceptor, the Voodoo has yet to meet its proven equal.

At this critical stage of the take-off, a Royal Canadian Air Force F-101B Voodoo pilot focuses complete attention to machine and mission.

Exposing its not-so-vulnerable underside to the camera, this Royal Canadian Air Force F-101B shows a keen eye two air-to-air Falcon missiles tucked away in the fuselage.

15

A McDonnell F-101C Voodoo of the Kentucky Air National Guard based at Louisville.

With drag chute deployed to help cut unwanted speed, this Royal Canadian Air Force F-101B
of 416 Squadron drops on its home runway.

Heading for high country, this F-101B from the 83rd Fighter Intercepter Squadron of the Air Defense Command begins a gradual left turn toward open Atlantic waters.

A dynamic duo of F-101Bs reach for the sky at K. I. Sawyer Air Force Base in Michigan.

An Illinois Air National Guard KC-97L takes on two thirsty customers high over its home state.

An F-105D from the 53rd Tactical Fighter Squadron of the 36th Tactical Fighter Wing based at Bitburg, Germany in January of 1962.

THE REPUBLIC F-105 THUNDERCHIEF

It has been said of Republic aircraft, that if the Air Force built a runway that stretched around the world and connected with itself, Republic could build an airplane that would use every inch of it to take-off. The P-47 Thunderbolt of World War II fame, the more recent F-84 Thunderstreak and now the F-105 Thunderchief all fall into the catagory of heavy-duty, maximum payload Republic ground-gainers.

Noted for its ability to deliver heavy payloads indigenous to a bomber and retain the performance of a fighter, the Thunderchief has been justly described as "the most powerful one-man airplane in the world." It is the first operational tactical-fighter-bomber combination incorporating electronic systems to provide automatic navigation, flight control and weapons delivery. In production form, the F-105 can fly a complete spectrum of missions with no less than 4,000 possible combinations of offensive weaponry, both conventional and nuclear.

Originally conceived as a private venture to succeed the aging F-84 Thunderstreak, the Thunderchief drew immediate government attention to its highly sophisticated integrated electronics systems. Because of the unavailability of higher powered engines, the first models of the Thunderchief were underpowered. Development of the Pratt and Whitney J75 gave the F-105 the zest it deserved.

21

The aircraft maintained an unusual safety record during trials and initial Air Defense Command deployment boasting a total of 12,326 accident-free hours. Deliveries began in 1959 with the first of the lot going to the crack 4th Fighter Wing based at Seymour-Johnson Air Force Base in North Carolina. Armed with a six-barrel 20 mm Vulcan gatling gun spraying 6,000 rounds per minute and many combinations of weaponry, the F-105 tips the scales at 40,000 pounds and can deliver its punch at twice the speed of sound. The intricate bird now staffs the Tactical Air Command and several Air National Guard Units.

On the Nellis Air Force Base flight line, a row of Thunderchiefs from the Tactical Air Command await the day's sorties.

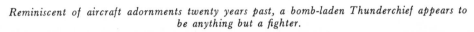

Reminiscent of aircraft adornments twenty years past, a bomb-laden Thunderchief appears to be anything but a fighter.

Above: With its turbines echoing their ear-piercing whine, a Republic F-105D is readied for airborne activities.

Right: Air-to-air refueling means work and lots of sweat, and that's not excepting this Republic F-105D jockey.

Left: Born to fight, these F-105D's roll down the assembly line at the Republic stables at Farmingdale, New York.

Below: A Thunderchief awaits the return of its lunch-bound handlers to complete minor repairs.

27

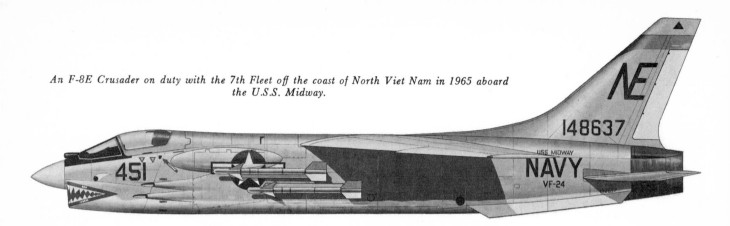

An F-8E Crusader on duty with the 7th Fleet off the coast of North Viet Nam in 1965 aboard the U.S.S. Midway.

THE LING-TEMCO-VOUGHT (CHANCE VOUGHT) F-8 CRUSADER

Whether the pilot of the Crusader flying from that Naval Base near Naples, Italy knew it or not, he was violating a Navy ordinance. He had taken off and climbed to 5,000 feet before he realized that he had done so with his wings in the folded position. Although the pilot's handbook for the Crusader sardonically states "it is customary to lower the wings prior to flight", the pilot had apparently overlooked the sarcasm of these words of wisdom.

When he tried to bend the nose over to level flight a mile up, he became concerned with the unusual amount of pressure required to maintain level flight. A quick glance over his shoulder was all that it took to make an old man out of him. He cooly decided to make the best of the situation by testing the flight characteristics while in the unusual configuration. He dumped fuel and returned for landing. When his bird was light enough for landing, he wisely planned the approach long and high. He crossed the fence at a quick 200 knots and got it stopped. The pilot walked away and later reported to several investigators that his forgiving bird was quite easy to handle during his hairy trip.

Aside from having the greatest wing area of any

28

fighter in service today, the most unique feature of the Crusader is its variable pitch wing. The entire wing is built as one unit and when pivoted back on a hinge, acts as a large flap to allow slower landing speeds and provide the pilot with visibility he needs in combination with the nose-high landing attitude on aircraft carriers.

Probably the most well-known record achieved by the Crusader was attained by Major J. H. Glenn (who later

Aboard the U.S.S. Forrestal, an F-8U Crusader is hooked to the steam catapult sling.

29

Right: The crew chief of this Crusader is helping his pilot become part of his machine at Marine Corps Air Station Roosevelt Roads in Puerto Rico.

Below: At Beaufort Marine Corps Air Station, an F-8U Crusader faces its replacement, an F-4C Phantom II, as the crack Marine unit updates its equipment.

became America's first globe-circling astronaut). In "Operation Bullet", Glenn won the Distinguished Flying Cross when he piloted a Crusader from California to New York in 203 minutes, averaging supersonic speed at 35,000 feet. In addition to the speed dash, his cameras on board took photos of every square foot of ground over which his aircraft traveled.

The famous Collier's Trophy was awarded to Ling-Temco-Vought in Dallas in 1958 for the most significant contribution to aviation — America's first 1,000 mile per hour fighter. Over 900 Crusaders equip both Navy and Marine squadrons today.

30

Right: The wisp of steam above the starboard catapult on the U.S.S. Enterprise traces the departure of Navy Commander Talley as he piloted the first aircraft to be slung off that nuclear aircraft carrier.

Below: After a low pass, the pilot of this photogenic Crusader lights the afterburner and looks for higher ground.

A Marine Crusader pilot shows every intention of snagging the second wire aboard the U.S.S. Forrestal.

THE CONVAIR F-106 DELTA DART

Almost as soon as the F-102 Delta Daggar was in full scale production and the Air Force began taking deliveries, engineers at Convair began work on a new and improved version to replace it. But as the new interceptor evolved with progressive changes in power, armament and systems, what was virtually a new aircraft began to emerge.

The F-106 Delta Dart is equipped with extremely advanced Hughes electronic and guidance components designed to serve the Air Defense Command. The basis behind the defense system is a digital computer with the pilot acting principally as a monitor with the ability to override the system in case of emergency. Once in combat radius, the Delta Dart's own radar detects the target and "locks on". The missiles launch automatically. The entire mission can be commanded from a ground post with the pilot only taking-off and landing the craft.

By comparison with the F-102 Delta Daggar, the Delta Dart has 50% more power, the engine air intakes are repositioned further back on the area ruled (coke bottle) fuselage, the delta wing is more swept and the bird is twice as fast.

Initial deliveries were made to the Air Defense Command in 1959 and by 1961, half of the Command's force had reequipped with the Dart. Since its debut, the Convair engineers have progressivly updated the F-106 in modernization programs which brought it up to final production standards.

The aircraft is provided with a supersonic ejection capsule. Normal fuel load is 1,200 gallons in two tanks

in each wing and one tank aft in the missile bay. For ferrying purposes or long range flights, two dropable 191 gallon tanks are attached to underwing pylons. Capable of two and one half times the speed of sound, the Delta Dart usually cruises at between fifty and seventy thousand feet. This aircraft remains the most sophisticated all weather interceptor employed by the armed forces.

Left: A pair of Delta Darts of the 498th Fighter Interceptor Squadron from McChord A.F.B. in Washington patrol high over Alaska on a routine mission.

Below: Resembling the F-102A Delta Daggar, the F-106 Delta Dart was designed as an improvement of the Daggar but the outcome proved to be an entirely different aircraft.

Above: On the ramp at Edwards Air Force Base in California, an F-106A of the Air Force Systems Command stands with its weapons bay open.

Left: Exposing the vent for its Pratt and Whitney powerplant, this F-106A from the 71st Fighter Interceptor Squadron stands empty weighing 26,000 pounds.

Triplet Delta Darts maintain tight formation on a routine sortie over the flatlands of central Kansas.

An F-104C of the 479th Tactical Fighter Wing.

THE LOCKHEED F-104 STARFIGHTER

Dubbed the "missile-with-a-man-in-it", the Lockheed F-104 Starfighter was born as one of the most significant developments of the 1950's. A cloak of controversy shrouded the Starfighter when, in original form, it proved to be somewhat of a disappointment. After an amazing metamorphosis from a short-range day fighter to an all-weather strike and reconnaissance aircraft, the F-104 was selected by the Tactical Air Command as *the* front-line fighter for scramble and intercept missions.

During flight tests in 1956, the Starfighter topped Mach 2.5 and climbed higher than 60,000 feet. This performance doubled the capability of the North American F-100 Super Sabre, then number one with T.A.C. In early 1958, Air Force Capt. Walter W. Irwin set a world speed record with a Starfighter when he scampered a zesty 1,404 miles per hour.

Characterized by its remarkably small wing area of 196 square feet, the F-104 incorporates boundary layer control. This relatively new innovation in aeronautics is the breakthrough that has made it possible for supersonic jet aircraft to maintain slow approach speeds for landing. Jets of air are blown across the wing and flap surfaces to 'trick' the wing into believing that it is flying faster than it is.

For an effective armament, Lockheed chose the Vulcan gatling cannon capable of spraying a dazzling 6,000 rounds per minute of 20 mm shells down the throat of the formidable foe. Four Sidewinder heat-seeking missiles add to the compliment of weapons. This firepower equaled ten times that deliverable by the North American P-51 Mustang of World War II fame.

Still in service with some units of the Air Defense 41

Command, the Starfighter is equipping many allies and NATO countries. The Chinese Nationalists Air Force, Japanese Air Force, Royal Canadian Air Force and some Air National Guard Units use the F-104 today.

Right: A quartet of Sidewinder-equipped F-104s self-consciously tighten their formation as they hurtle through the Golden Gate on their way back to the 83rd Fighter Intercepter Base.

Below: With his crew chief close at his heels, this F-104 Starfighter pilot scrambles into his home away from home and will soon identify what the radar boys couldn't.

Capable of attaining altitudes exceeding 125,000 feet, this rocket-boosted F-104A is attached to the Aerospace Research Pilot's School at Edwards A.F.B.

Above: This bombed-up F-104G fighter-bomber displays the extreme versatility of the original Starfighter design.

Right: The serene atmosphere around this Canadian farmhouse is about to be shattered by a foursome of Maple Leaf standardbearers.

46

The YF-12A as it appeared in its initial rollout for the news media.

THE LOCKHEED YF-12A

In 1958, designers and engineers from Boeing, North American, General Dynamics and Lockheed went to Washington with briefcases handcuffed to their arms. In them were blueprints of an aircraft designed to fly three times the speed of sound at above 70,000 feet with fuel making possible a round trip from England to Moscow. Behind closed doors at the Central Intelligence Agency in a cloak of secrecy, the Lockheed Aircraft Company was given the nod.

Clarence L. Johnson of Lockheed's Burbank plant, a co-designer of the Constellation airliner, went home to the same drawing boards that spawned his hunch-back airliner of twenty years past. Working for nearly five years, the men at Burbank gave the United States the A-11. The confirmation of unusual occurances at Edwards Air Test Center came in February of 1964 when President Johnson unveiled the advanced aircraft and its intended role as a spy in the sky.

Flight testing of the two-seat all-weather aircraft began in 1965 by the U.S.A.F. Strategic Air Command and soon thereafter it was announced that the titanium A-11 was no longer an unarmed spy but an interceptor called the YF-12A. Equipped with a fire control missile system developed by the Hughes Tool Company married to four Hughes Falcon missiles, the $25 million YF-12A has gone into service with S.A.C at Beale Air Force Base in California.

With the tactical designation SR-71, the Air Force has taken pride in establishing several world speed and altitude records formerly held by the Soviet Union. Verified by the International Aeronautical Federation in Paris, a record set by Col. Robert L. Stephens and Lt. Col. Daniel Andre clocked 2,062 miles per hour and saw the SR-71 top 100,000 feet.

Orders for no less than fifty aircraft have been placed by the Air Force.

48

The February 1964 announcement by the Chief Executive confirmed suspicions of unusual occurrences at Edwards Flight Test Center, and for most, beyond their wildest expectations.

49

Looking like anything but a fighter, the 2,000 mile per hour YF-12A is in service with the Strategic Air Command at Beale A.F.B. in California.

An F-102A from the 32nd Fighter Squadron while based at Soesterberg, Holland in 1962.

THE CONVAIR F-102 DELTA DAGGAR

By late 1951, a new shape in the fighter breed was spawned on the drawing boards at the Convair Aircraft Company in San Diego. Relying heavily on what the Germans had learned from testing the triangular-shaped wing during World War II, Convair engineers were well on the way to delivering the free world's first fighter/interceptor with a delta wing design.

High hopes resulting from optimistic wind tunnel results were clouded when the prototype YF-102 failed to reach the expected high speeds earlier forseen. All contracts for the F-102 were cancelled by the Air Force but the atmosphere at Convair was not entirely despondent. The model had the most powerful engine available in the West. Convair maintained hope that if drag could

be reduced on the aircraft, an exceptional fighter would result. Extensive modification was started and within a year the F-102 had been "cleaned up" with an area ruled (coke bottle curve) fuselage, a sharper nose, a knife-edge canopy and smaller engine intakes. This did the trick.

Air Force specifications called for the F-102 to act as a 'flying platform' for the Hughes Tool Company's computerized missile intercept control system. The aircraft and system were mated and immediately placed in service with the Air Defense Command, thus making the Delta Daggar the first fighter to dispense completely with a fixed gun armament.

The Hughes system uses six air-to-air guided missiles **51** with a secondary barage of twenty-four unguided heat-seeking missiles. Development of the advanced system enabled ground controllers to 'fly' the F-102 to a suspected target by relating headings to the aircraft's computer.

A twin seat F-102 designed as a trainer attained success with squadrons operating the fighter version as a proficiency tutor. Today, the 900 mile-per-hour fighter is in service with the U.S.A.F. in the Pacific and in Europe as well as staffing many National Guard Units.

Providing a two-pronged air defense for the Alaskan skies, member of the 31st and 317th Fighter Interceptor Squadrons stationed at Elmendorf A.F.B. sweep across the Chugach mountain range in Alaska.

Freshly adorned in colors indicative of subterfuge, a brace of F-102 Delta Daggars depart San Diego for points west.

An F-102A of the 4780th Air Defense Wing at Perrin Air Force Base, Texas, walks before it can run.

High over their native state, a pair of South Carolina Air National Guard members hold a loose formation in their F-102As.

Above: High over Houston and climbing, this trio of F-102 Delta Daggers is attached to the 149th Fighter Group otherwise known as the Texas Air National Guard.

Left: A member of the South Carolina's Air National Guard Squadron stands only minutes from living up to its role as an interceptor.

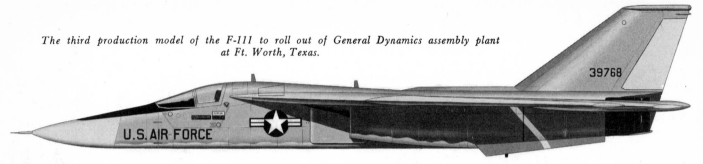

The third production model of the F-111 to roll out of General Dynamics assembly plant at Ft. Worth, Texas.

THE GENERAL DYNAMICS F-111

When the Pentagon laid down the requirements for the TFX (Tactical Fighter Experimental), engineers and designers from the major aircraft manufacturers looked at each other in bewilderment. Since the word 'impossible' isn't in an engineer's vocabulary, only the facial expression registered what was thought.

Both the Navy and the Air Force wanted a multi-purpose fighter that would fly two and one half times the speed of sound in a high altitude dash, one and one half times the speed of sound at low level, the ability to take-off and land over a 50-foot obstacle from 3,000 feet of runway, suitability for operation from short, rough, unimproved landing strips near front lines, a 4,000 mile range to enable it to fly anywhere in the world between two airfields in one day, a five to six hour 'loiter' capability over a target and a landing speed not to exceed 115 knots! What an order. Aside from these specifications, a high degree of commonality was demanded between versions of the two services.

It became immediately obvious that any airplane capable of fulfilling all of these requirements could only be produced if a practical variable-geometry wing could be evolved. The development of such a wing represented the greatest advance in the past decade in the field of airframe design.

General Dynamics was awarded the contract in 1962 with Grumman Aircraft of Bethpage, New York as associate builder of the Navy model. Initial contracts called for twenty-three aircraft, eighteen of which were to go to the Air Force. The first aircraft flew in 1964 with success. A few weeks later, another aircraft was tested utilizing the variable-geometry wing.

Two Pratt and Whitney TF-30 turbofans power the unusual fighter at better than Mach 2.5. The maximum gross weight of 69,000 pounds is more than three fully loaded DC-3s. Defense Department cutbacks and cancellation of many defense programs is proof enough that the expectation of the aircraft will be met and that the F-111 will serve as the front-line tactical fighter/bomber for the duration of the sixties.

The world's first production aircraft with variable sweep wings, the General Dynamics F-111 meets the press at a rollout ceremony at the Ft. Worth, Texas plant.

In another rollout ceremony 1,500 miles away, the Grumman Aircraft corporation introduced the Navy version of the bi-service F-111 in Long Island, New York.

After much controversy, the General Dynamics F-111 was given the nod to enter service as a tactical fighter-bomber, thus aging the talents of the B-58 Hustler and B-52 Stratofortress.

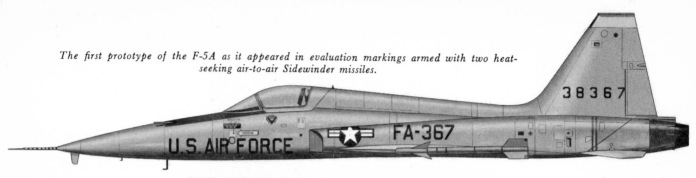

The first prototype of the F-5A as it appeared in evaluation markings armed with two heat-seeking air-to-air Sidewinder missiles.

THE NORTHROP F-5A FREEDOM FIGHTER

The first U.S. post-war combat aircraft designed specifically to meet the requirements of foreign air arms rather than for a specialized U.S.A.F. military need, the Northrop F-5 is being supplied to small N.A.T.O. and S.E.A.T.O. air mights. The training and indoctrination of these foreign pilots is done at Williams Air Force Base, Arizona where aircraft delivery is made.

Development of the Freedom Fighter began in 1954 when a team from Northrop toured N.A.T.O. and S.E.A.T.O. countries to determine the need to satisfy the obligation. The result of the survey called for a relatively simple, economical and versatile light aircraft suitable for strike, attack, intercept and reconnaissance missions. Powered by twin General Electric J-85s, the F-5 first flew in 1959. Initial orders exceeded 160 machines.

The first recipient of the Freedom Fighter was the Royal Hellenic Air Force which took delivery of forty. The Royal Norwegian Air Force took sixty-five. Two Browning 20 mm cannons and a maximum ordnance load of 6,000 pounds gives the Mach 1.2 fighter a punch hereinbefore absent from foreign air forces.

A typical firepower load carried by the F-5 Freedom Fighter would consist of two Sidewinder air-to-missiles, one 2,000 pound general purpose bomb, two 1,000 pound general purpose bombs, two 75 pound incendiary bombs and two Bullpup air-to-surface missiles.

Exceptionally well powered, the F-5 has shaken the record books with its performance as an interceptor. The fantastic climb rate is indicated when the bird goes from 'brakes off' to 40,000 feet in a scant four minutes and eighteen seconds.

With the introduction of air-to-air and air-to-ground radar, the all-weather capabilities of the F-5 Freedom Fighter are pronounced. Infrared sensing lends the fighter to serving its master night or day, rain or shine.

The U.S. is operationally checking the F-5 in Viet Nam in its "Skoshi Tiger" program. Results from the evaluations are exceeding all expectations in overall performance.

Developed to satisfy the needs of the North Atlantic Treaty Organization's members, the Northrop F-5 is the first U.S. post-war combat aircraft designed specifically for foreign air arms rather than for a U.S. military requirement.

Right: Adorned in three-toned camouflage, an F-5 drinks thirstily high over Arizona from a KC-135 tanker while two cohorts wait their turn. The aircraft are flown by pilots from the 4503rd Tactical Fighter Squadron.

Below: Capable of nearly twice the speed of sound, the F-5's dual General Eelectric turbojets hurtle pilot and machine through 40,000 feet a scant 4.3 minutes after take-off roll.

Armed with heat-seeking Sidewinder missiles, a patrol of F-5 Freedom Fighters maintain close watch.

The prototype A-7A Corsair II as it appeared during rollout at the Ling-Temco-Vought plant in Dallas in October, 1965.

THE LING-TEMCO-VOUGHT A-7A CORSAIR II

As the son of the F-8U Crusader, the Ling-Temco-Vought A-7A Corsair II has a family reputation to uphold and a man-size job facing it. Designed as the successor to the Douglas A-4 Skyhawk attack bomber, the Corsair II is an abbreviated subsonic version of the F-8U Crusader, backbone of the Navy's air arm. Measuring half as long and weighing nearly the same as the Crusader, the Corsair II will carry a bomb load in excess of 9,500 pounds.

Engineers at Ling-Temco-Vought in Dallas designed the single-seat fighter to offer twice the effectiveness of the A-4 Skyhawk on short-range missions and four times the punch on longer sorties. Not only differing from its father in weight and length, the Corsair II does not incorporate the 'pop up' variable incidence wing used for slow approaches to aircraft carriers.

Two 20 mm cannons are mounted in the ship's nose and a lightweight advanced electronics system is installed for attack missions.

Scheduled to enter operational service with the U.S. Navy in 1967, the A-7A Corsair II will be required to undergo shipborne trials prior to Navy acceptance and subsequent ordering. The contract states that the Corsair II will attain 80% effectiveness on mission tests and that no less than 20 maintenance hours per flying hour be encountered during the tests series.

67

Riding with the name of Corsair, the A-7A tradition dates back to World War II when the Chance Vought Corsair (later merged to form Ling-Temco-Vought) won fame in the Pacific skies operating from unimproved airfields and aircraft carriers against the Japanese. The gull-wing Corsair established a name for itself among Navy pilots — one that will take another superior machine to equal.

The Ling-Temco-Vought A-7A Corsair II was designed as a successor to the Douglas A-4 Skyhawk and upon completion met the immediate approval of the Navy.

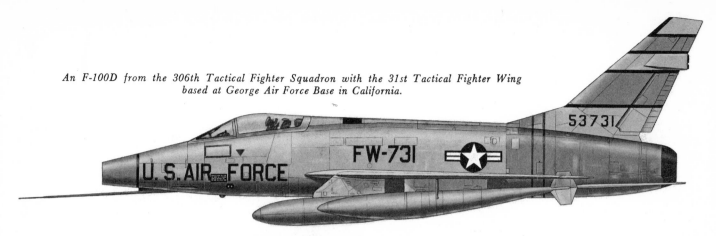

An F-100D from the 306th Tactical Fighter Squadron with the 31st Tactical Fighter Wing based at George Air Force Base in California.

THE NORTH AMERICAN F-100 SUPER SABRE

As the first of the "Century Series" fighters, the North American F-100 Super Sabre was the first free-world aircraft to fly faster than the speed of sound in level flight for extended periods.

Development of the Super Sabre began in 1949, but the first aircraft did not fly until 1953. By late 1954, the Air Force had placed orders totalling $1 billion for the Super Sabre and its continued development. Initial deliveries of the aircraft went to the 479th Fighter Wing at George Air Force Base in California.

Unfortunate luck saw a trio of accidents involving the F-100 after deliveries began, one killing North American's chief test pilot, George Welch. The Air Force grounded the Super Sabre and a detailed investigation followed. After over 3,000 hours of research, it was determined that there was an aerodynamic failing of the vertical stabilizer during a roll.

The fin was redesigned with added area and the wing span was increased by two feet. Despite the lengthy delay for modification of all aircraft, the Super Sabre was again in service by 1955. When the basic design was proven sound, the engineers went back to work on testing to increase the versatility of the aircraft.

Eight underwing pylons were added to maximize the 69

A droop-snoot F-100 Super Sabre tucks up its feet and points its candy-striped pitot tube toward high country. The same California stables bred the B-25 Mitchell, the AT-6 Harvard, the P-51 Mustang and the F-86 Sabre.

useful load of weaponery at 7,500 pounds. A Minneapolis-Honeywell autopilot, expressly designed for supersonic jets, and an automatic fire control intercept system were installed to render the pilot free to make an intercept or precision bombing run.

Capable of speeds in excess of 800 miles per hour, the Super Sabre is fitted with autoslats, a carry-over from the F-86, which enable the pilot to execute a complete roll in one second. The aircraft lands at 130 miles per hour and a drag chute is required for braking. Before a pilot can fly the F-100, about 100 hours are required in the F-86 Sabre with transition taking 10 hours.

In a unique test flight out of Edwards Air Test Center, a McDonnell RF-101 Voodoo trails a drogue for an F-100 Super Sabre in a fighter-to-fighter refueling operation.

Right: As observed from a KB-50 tanker, an F-100 jockey takes aim on his source for his machine's life blood.

Below: As the first of the "Century Series", the F-100 was the first production fighter designed to fly faster than the speed of sound for sustained periods.

Above: With the Colorado mountains echoing their afterburning thunder, the Air Force Thunderbird Exhibition Team drop lower than the Air Force Academy's 400 foot Chapel steeple to demonstrate their aerial artistry.

Right: With everything out, this F-100D from the 354th Tactical Fighter Wing at Myrtle Beach Air Force Base rolls onto final approach.

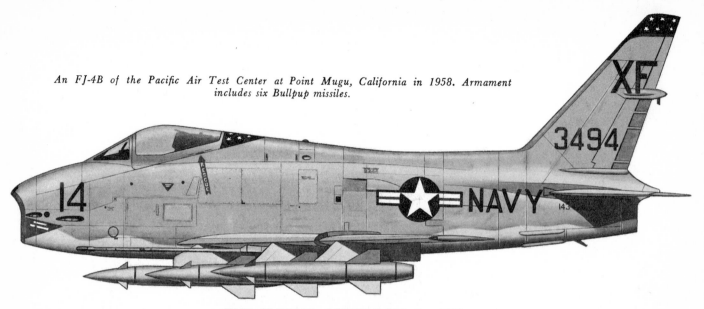

An FJ-4B of the Pacific Air Test Center at Point Mugu, California in 1958. Armament includes six Bullpup missiles.

THE NORTH AMERICAN FJ FURY

A derivative of the F-86 Sabre of Korean War fame, the North American FJ Fury is a redesigned version of the Sabre adaptable for operations from the deck of an aircraft carrier with the Navy. Initial sea trials exposed unsuitable traits and as the Navy cancelled their orders, the Marines took over the program and gave the Fury new life. Although developed quickly, the Fury was too late for any great impact on the Korean war.

As that War dragged on in the early fifties, the Marine Corps achieved a major first when on July 11, 1953, Lt. Col. John F. Bolt became the first jet ace in the Corp's history. He shot down his fifth and sixth Mig 15s while leading a four plane flight east of Sinuiju.

As the pilot of this FJ Fury hurridly runs through his "before take-off" checklist, deck hands move clear of the aircraft that they have just latched onto the ship's steam catapult.

Modifications and powerplant revisions caused the Navy to re-examine the previously rejected Fury. Trials were done aboard the U.S.S. Bennington and incorporated three Furies. Each pilot of the ship's squadron made three landings and take-offs. Four days later after 180 sorties, the Navy bought the Fury.

The Fury has a normal armament of four 20 mm cannons in her nose. Auxiliary underwing dropable fuel tanks increased her range by 1,500 miles and provisions for inflight refueling added to her distance. Normally, the Fury operates below 50,000 feet at 650 miles per hour. Underwing pylons carry Sidewinder missiles.

Intentional spins are prohibited in the Fury. Once in a spin, a single turn could cost the pilot 2,700 feet and a minimum of 7,000 feet was required to effect recovery. Navy orders were to eject should a spin occur below that altitude. It has been said that the Fury taught the Navy its first real experience with high speed jet aircraft.

Designed as a day interceptor, attack and light bomber, the Fury has played that role for nearly ten years. With the Phantom, Crusader and Demon on deck, the aircraft has been relegated to the Naval Air Training Command and to some Marine and Naval Reserve units.

Bearing a close resemblance to its sister, the North American F-86 Sabre of the Korean War fame, the FJ Fury was adopted by the Navy for carrier based operations.

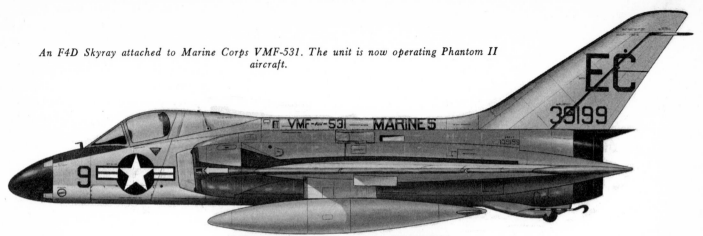

An F4D Skyray attached to Marine Corps VMF-531. The unit is now operating Phantom II aircraft.

THE DOUGLAS F-6A SKYRAY

As with most Douglas aircraft, the F-6A Skyray proved itself a pilot's airplane from its inception. Not only appealing in appearance, the Skyray maintained the appreciation and respect of all who flew her when she was a front-line interceptor with the Navy in the late fifties. Now relegated for service with the Naval Air Training Command and Naval Reserve units, the Skyray possesses the unique distinction of being the only Navy aircraft to staff a vital position in the North American Air Defense Command, an honor normally comprised of U.S.A.F. formations.

Douglas test pilot Robert O. Rahn achieved supersonic flight on the Skyray's maiden voyage. Navy officials showed enthusiasm in the 'sting ray' resembling aircraft when they signed checks for 420 aircraft. Few modifications were made on the initial design and in 1956 the first delivery was made.

Impressive records were assaulted by Skyray pilots within the first months of its active service record. Bi-war veteran Major E. N. Faivre challenged the world's official climb record and ended up breaking five records in the process.

Impressive performance led to the Skyray's assignment for use in the envied North American Air Defense Command. Capable of supersonic speeds as a matter of course above 40,000 feet, the Skyray can carry an assortment of armament which usually includes four 20 mm cannons and a weapon load exceeding 7,000 pounds including infrared Sidewinder missiles.

The distinctive design of the Skyray would seemingly be dubbed a delta configuration, but Douglas engineers say no. Powered by a General Electric J57 turbojet, the Skyray played an active part in the nation's defense with both the Navy and the Marines until it was replaced by the Phantom II, the Crusader and the Demon.

An attempt to sell the Navy on a revised, more powerful version of the Skyray as an all-weather interceptor came to an abrupt halt in 1956. The updated Skylancer proved indeed to be superior to its predecessor in both performance and appearance but the project was cancelled through lack of funds.

Left: The Douglas F-6A Skyray was developed in the early 1950s as a carrier based supersonic interceptor fighter. Now obsolete as a front-line interceptor, the Skyray is used extensively with the Training Command and in Navy and Marine Reserve units.

Below: At El Toro Marine Corps Air Station, a quartet of F-6A Skyrays bask in the warm California sun.

81

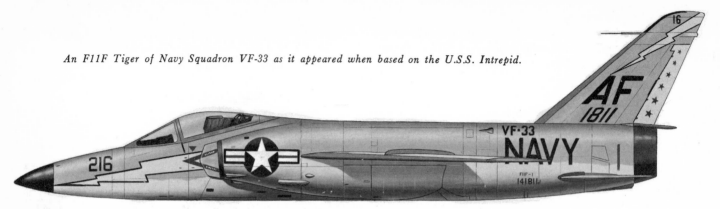

An F11F Tiger of Navy Squadron VF-33 as it appeared when based on the U.S.S. Intrepid.

THE GRUMAN F11A TIGER

The last of the fighter breed to emerge from the Grumman Aircraft plant in New York was the F11F Tiger. Not unlike other fighters that had teethed during the fifties, the Tiger fell short of its intended goal. When it was proved that the bird would not live up to its role as a lightweight fighter/interceptor for the Navy, Grumman engineers went back to work. Three years of redesigning and modification produced what the Navy had ordered, and then some.

Power for the Tiger came in the form of a Wright Aircraft Company turbojet delivering 11,300 pounds of thrust with afterburner. The Tiger was ready for a second try. During initial armament tests, Grumman pilot Tom Attridge fell prey to the revamped cat's latent abilities.

At 40,000 feet over Long Island on September 21, 1956, Attridge shot himself down when he crossed a spray of 20 mm shells he had just fired!

First speed trials credited the Tiger with a top hustle of 950 miles per hour and a climb rate exceeding 18,000 feet per minute. With this performance, the Navy had its first aircraft that could travel faster than the speed of sound in level flight. A total of 198 Tigers were delivered, a team of which are used by the Naval aerobatic demonstration squad, the Blue Angels.

Later modifications and the addition of more armament and dropable fuel tanks dictated a search for more power. General Electric's J79 was given the nod. During testing phases at Edwards Air Test Center, an attempt at the speed record was tried. An unofficial 1,220 miles per hour was attained and within three days, Lt. Cmdr. G. C. Watkins of the Navy reached 72,000 feet. Two days later, Watkins topped 76,500 feet in the same aircraft, and was still climbing.

Under Mutual Defense Aid contracts, the Grumman Company produced the F11F Tiger for the Japanese Air Force. The potent Tiger still flies with the Navy today but is active only with Reserve units.

The world famous Blue Angels Navy Demonstration Team using Grumman F11A Tigers pay an aerial salute to the great lady in New York harbor.

84

As part of their demonstration of precision flying, the Blue Angels in their Grumman Tigers fly in the diamond formation with the flight leader inverted. The Team has performed before an estimated 76 million people.

An F3H Demon attached to Navy Squadron VF-114 as it appeared when aboard the U.S.S. Forrestal.

THE McDONNELL M-3B DEMON

Owing its inception and service requirements to the harried and troubled times of the early fifties, the McDonnell Demon probably holds the record for the shortest time to travel from drawing board to runway — two years. The clean and appealing lines of the Demon took shape at the McDonnell Aircraft plant in St. Louis in 1949 as part of a Navy order for an all-weather fighter/interceptor with provisions for delivering a barrage of heat-seeking Sidewinder missiles.

Under the pressure of the Korean War, the Navy Department ordered nearly 150 Demons as the probable answer to the Mig 15 should the war drag on. It became evident after the first production model had flown that the aircraft was sadly underpowered and could not meet

the basic requirements set forth by the Navy. Working feverishly on modifications, the engineers at McDonnell were further hampered when the lives of three of their test pilots were taken in proving runs. The aircraft was grounded three years after the first pencils were sharpened.

Westinghouse, designer and builder of the not-so-popular J40 turbojet engine, was asked to halt production of that powerplant and the Allison company was given a contract to develop the J71. The Demon was refitted amid Congressional investigation of the project's failure and for the first time since its inception, the aircraft performed as expected. The Defense Secretary summed the project up by saying, "None of the parties could really be blamed. The M-3B was a crash program, and

whenever several models are rushed into production, you occasionally get a sour one."

But now a sour one it is not. The Demon serves the Navy's best carriers as an interceptor. With an initial climb rate of over 12,000 feet per minute and supersonic speed, the Demon has gained a number of world "firsts". It is the first Navy jet to fly from the U.S. to England and the first to test fire the Sparrow missile. In spite of its inauspicious start, the Demon flys with the Navy's air arm as a vital part of the nation's defense.

Left: Leaving an aircraft carrier via the canted deck, an F-3H Demon rotates and heads for open water. Note the pilot's canopy remains open for quick evacuation should the Demon encounter trouble at this critical stage of flight.

Below: The firey fingers of flame from two McDonnell F-3H Demons lick the deck of the U.S.S. Forrestal as their nocturnal pilots go into full afterburner for a night intercept.

An F-89J with the 126th Fighter Squadron designated the Wisconsin Air National Guard

THE NORTHROP F-89 SCORPION

During its heyday in the mid fifties, the Northrop F-89 Scorpion was primarily an interceptor with the Air Defense Command, but has now taken a second row seat to progress and is all but phased out and ready for the scrap heap. Still serving with Air National Guard units, the F-89 once stood the alerts now staffed with Phantom IIs, Thunderchiefs and Delta Darts.

Adding a nuclear punch and cleaning her up for a few knots more speed kept the Scorpion alive for several years after she was destined for the torch but finally the race with technology caught up with her. The subsonic twin-engine, two place interceptor once scanned the North American skies from Alaska to Newfoundland and along the Distant Early Warning Line for almost a decade to intercept and ward off possible enemy attack.

But now her wing tip pods are used for fuel tanks and are no longer equipped to unleash forty-two 2.75 inch missiles in one flash. Genie air-to-ground unguided missiles once dropped from her straight midwings but now only the pylons remember.

Twin Allison join efforts to give the Scorpion 5,400 horsepower or that comparable to a DC-4 airliner. Operating at a normal cruise setting of nearly 500 miles per hour, the Scorpion has a useful range of nearly 1,700 miles without refueling.

Today, weekend warriors staff the cockpits of the Scorpion and the closest that the aircraft will ever get to the old days will be at a summer camp where her

National Guard charges will occasionally give her a low-level straffing run or maybe a practice skirmish with another group.

For the most part, Air National Guard Units are being reequipped with F-102 Delta Daggars, F-101 Voodoos and F-104 Starfighters so only a matter of time stands between the grand lady and a final resting place in the Air Force Museum. Some will go to the front yards of small town city halls, others will stand majestically atop concrete pillars at Air Force Bases that once used her and the rest will be melted to scrap.

Two "Happy Holligans" from the North Dakota Air National Guard prepare for a sortie in their Northrop F-89J Scorpion. With an external power unit doing its part, only RPMs separate this bird from the Dakota skies.

The Northrop F-89J Scorpion has taken a back seat to the Convair F-102 Delta Daggar in most Air Guard Units. Some still operate the 1950 vintage all-weather interceptor as do these Montana pilots.

An F-86L of the 194th Air National Guard Fighter Interceptor Squadron as seen at Oxnard Air Force Base air show in the fall 1964.

THE NORTH AMERICAN F-86D SABRE

Of all the contemporary fighter aircraft, the one most assured of a place in aviation's hall of fame with the other great warplanes of the world is the North American F-86 Sabre. Although it is twenty years young, the Sabre is still an important front-line fighter with air forces of smaller countries as well as staffing the Air National Guard Units of several states. Even the experts are reluctant to measure the time until this amazing little fighter will make its last landing and become another of aviation's immortals.

The lineage of the Sabre dates back to the end of World War II when Western engineers began to realize the vital research conducted by the Germans on swept wing aircraft design. The first example flew in 1948 and astounded observers with its initial performance. By the end of 1949, the crack 1st Fighter Group was completely equipped with the Sabre. The Korean War gave the bird a shot of vitamin that it didn't need. As the answer to the Mig 15, the Sabre played its expected instrumental role in aerial warfare during the conflict.

The advent of the F-86 was the climax of an exploitation of the proven design of the basic Sabre model. Virtually a new and different aircraft, the "Dog" was an all-weather interceptor with a highly sophisticated electronics system married to guided misiles. Contracts were awarded for the F-86D in 1950 and by 1952, modification of 2,500 aircraft was completed.

Powered by a General Electric J47 turbojet with afterburner, the "Dog" cruised at 700 miles per hour at 40,000 feet, optimum performance for radar intercept missions. All of the teething problems were quickly ironed out in the F-86D once it became active with the Air Force. Because of its advanced electronics systems, pilots required more training on the aircraft than with any other U.S.A.F. fighter.

Air Forces now equipped with the F-86D include Royal Netherlands, Turkish Air Force, Philippine Air Force, Chinese Nationaiists Air Force, Yugoslav Air Force, Royal Hellenic Air Force, German Luftwaffe, Republic of Korea Air Force and the Japanese Air Force. Some National Guard units still operate the Sabre.

Right: High over the flat west Texas prairie, a lone member of the Texas Air National Guard heads for the barn after a routine sortie. The state has now traded all of its F-86Ds for F-102 Delta Daggars.
Below: Weekend warriors from some states still operate these North American F-86Ds but for the most part have made the transition to F-102, F-104 or F-105 aircraft.

An F-84F Thunderstreak of the 183rd Tactical Fighter Group designated the Illinois Air National Guard based at Springfield, Illinois.

THE REPUBLIC F-84F THUNDERSTREAK

Having the unique distinction of being one of the only aircraft ever to have the same designation and appear as more than one basic design, the Republic F-84 is three separate aircraft in one. The original F-84 Thunderjet, which is no longer in service with U.S. units, incorporated a straight wing design and was the first single-seat fighter/bomber in the U.S.A.F. capable of handling a tactical atomic weapon. The next in line, the F-84 Thunderstreak, features the same fuselage as its predecessor but has swept wings and is nearly twice as fast. The third model F-84 is merely a derivative

of the Thunderstreak. The RF-84F Thunderflash is camera laden for reconnaissance missions. To accomplish this, Republic enclosed the nose and modified the wing roots for the jet intakes. The Thunderflash is basically the same as its sister, the Thunderstreak.

Owing its inception and success to the Korean War, the F-84 series now staffs air forces including North Korean, German, Netherlands, Belgian, Italian, Turkish, French and Japanese. It took the hostilities in Korea to impress military decision-makers with Republic's design. No fewer than 2,700 were ordered.

94

The first production model of the Thunderstreak was delivered to the Air Force in 1952 to the Tactical Air Command. Not unlike other Republic aircraft including the P-47 Thunderbolt and the F-105 Thunderchief, the F-84 Thunderstreaks and Thunderflashes are sticklers for using every inch of runway to take-off. One pilot flying F-84s noted a revision that his squadron had made on its aircraft to improve take-off acceleration. A small bag of sand was allegedly installed (and refilled after every take-off) in the nosewheel well and jettisoned in

A Republic Aviation F-84F Thunderstreak remembers younger days as she stands close to retirement in the hands of only a few National Guard units.

front of the tire on take-off roll. The intended result was to trick the nosewheel into thinking that it had used up all of the runway and was starting down the overrun at the end. Hence, flight.

Although subsonic, the Thunderstreak/Thunderflash is hot on the approach with a sizzling 155 miles per hour. This habit gained the respect of many Air Force pilots who had the pleasure of flying her.

A hybrid of the F-84F Thunderstreak, this RF-84F reconnaissance version is known as a Thunderflash. This variant also remembers brighter days before the Alabama Air Guard flew the last bit of life out of her. She too is destined for the scrap heap.

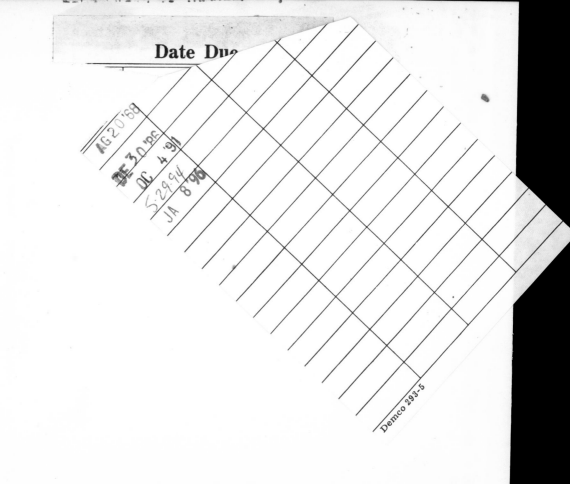

Date Due

AG 20 '68
DE 30 '86
OC 4 '91
5-29-94
JA 8 96

Demco 293-5